LETTERS HOME from ZION

Lisa Halvorsen

BLACKBIRCH PRESS, INC.

WOODBRIDGE, CONNECTICUT

Published by Blackbirch Press, Inc.
260 Amity Road
Woodbridge, CT 06525

©2000 by Blackbirch Press, Inc.
First Edition

e-mail: staff@blackbirch.com
Web site: www.blackbirch.com

Printed in Singapore

10 9 8 7 6 5 4 3 2 1

All photographs ©Corel Corporation, except page 29 (left): ©Joyce and Frank
Burek/Earth Scenes.

Library of Congress Cataloging-in-Publication Data
Halvorsen, Lisa.
Zion / by Lisa Halvorsen.
    p.   cm. — (Letters home from national parks)
Includes index.
Summary: This first-person account of a trip to Zion National Park describes some of its
outstanding features, including colorful canyons, the Virgin River, trails, and strange rock
formations..
ISBN 1-56711-464-4 (alk. paper)
1. Zion National Park (Utah)—Juvenile literature. [1. Zion National Park (Utah)
2. National parks and reserves.] I. Title
F832.Z8 H35 2000
979.2'48—cd21   00-008125

TABLE OF CONTENTS

Arrival in . . .

Las Vegas

I can't believe how awesome Zion National Park is! We just got here this morning, after a 3-hour drive from the Las Vegas airport.

I read that Zion is Utah's oldest national park. It is located in the southwestern corner of the state on the edge of the Colorado Plateau.

According to my guidebook, many Native Americans, including the Pueblo and Paiute, lived here many years ago. The first white person to visit the area was a Mormon scout named Nephi Johnson in 1858. He was sent by Brigham Young, leader of the Mormon church, to find a place for a new settlement. The Mormons called the area Zion, which means "heavenly place."

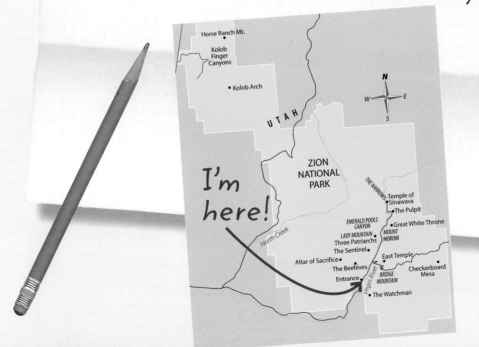

Virgin River

We entered through the southern entrance, where the Watchman guards the 229-square-mile park. This jagged peak is 6,555 feet tall. If you hiked to its peak, you'd have a great view of Zion Canyon, which was carved out by the North Fork of the Virgin River almost 13 million years ago! The canyon walls go straight up into the sky for almost half a mile.

No one is exactly sure how the river got its name. Some people believe Spanish explorers named it "Río Virgen" after the Virgin Mary. Others think it was named for Thomas Virgin, an American who explored the park.

The Watchman

Virgin River

I read that the Virgin River has been called a "moving river of sandpaper." That's because the water action constantly eats away the canyon walls. I was amazed to learn that every day the river moves about 180 carloads of gravel out of the park!

Bridge Mountain

Later the same day, we followed the Zion-Mt. Carmel scenic byway from Zion Canyon to the eastern entrance of the park. We had to drive slowly because the road has many switchbacks.

The road also tunnels through the side of the 6,803-foot-high Bridge Mountain. The mountain was named for the natural arch high on its face. The tunnel is more than 1 mile long and was blasted out of solid sandstone.

Bridge Mountain

Bridge Mountain

Checkerboard Mesa

Just before we got to the eastern entrance, we stopped at the Canyon Overlook. There, we followed a short, rocky trail above Pine Creek. The view was unbelievable. We got a good look at East Temple and, in the far distance, the Towers of the Virgin.

We also saw a strange geological formation along this road. Checkerboard Mesa is a rust-and-sand-colored dome that looks like a big checkerboard! The ranger told us that it is a petrified dune of Navajo sandstone, the most common rock in the park. It is 2,000 feet thick. This type of rock is often called slickrock.

Checkerboard Mesa

Towers of the Virgin

East Temple

Once we arrived at the eastern entrance, we retraced our route back to the Virgin River and Zion Canyon. I loved watching the herds of mule deer and the bighorn sheep grazing along the roadside.

Back in Zion Canyon, we jumped on the shuttle bus to take in the sights along the 7-mile-long scenic drive. The road actually follows the Virgin River through the canyon.

Twin Brothers and East Temple

East Temple

East Temple

Mount Spry and East Temple

Our first stop was East Temple. Our guide told us about a geologist named Charles Dutton. He gave East Temple its name in 1882. He also named West Temple. It is believed to be one of the tallest sandstone cliffs in the world!

Our guidebook says that many millions of years ago, West Temple and East Temple were joined together. Over time, wind, rain, and frost wore away the rock that connected them.

Beehives and Altar of Sacrifice

Next we saw the Beehives. They are more than 6,900 feet high! These formations were named by Mormon pioneers. They believed the beehive represented hard work, so they adopted it as their symbol. Our guide told us that the official nickname of Utah is the "Beehive State."

We saw our first hoodoo near the Beehives. This funny name refers to a column of eroded rock that has a cap of more resistant rock. Many hoodoos have weird shapes.

The Beehives

The Beehives

To the west, we could see the Altar of Sacrifice. It is a massive white cliff stained with red patches of iron oxide that has seeped out of the rock layers. If you use your imagination, the red looks like blood. No wonder they call the cliff the Altar of Sacrifice!

Our driver shared some park history as we drove toward the Sentinel. Around 1900, an artist named Frederick Dellenbaugh painted scenes of Zion Canyon. These paintings were shown at the 1904 World's Fair in St. Louis, Missouri. Public interest in Zion prompted President William Taft to declare the area a national monument in 1909. It was first called Mukuntuweap National Monument. Mukuntuweap is a Paiute word for "straight river."

Altar of Sacrifice

The Sentinel

Around the next bend we spotted the Twin Brothers and Mountain of the Sun. This mountain got its name because its peak catches the first rays of sun in the morning and the last light at night. I can just imagine what Mountain of the Sun looks like at dawn. The valley between the two is called a hanging valley. That's because the valley floor is higher than the main canyon floor. These hanging valleys are connected by waterfalls with the river below.

The Sentinel has a sharp, rocky summit. I read in my guidebook that this 7,157-foot-high mountain was first climbed in 1938.

The Sentinel

Monkey Flowers and Shooting Stars

Almost 800 native species of plants grow inside the park. That's more than 70% of all the native plants found in Utah. Wildflowers, such as golden columbines, monkey flowers, shooting stars, and evening primroses thrive here. Even orchids grow in moist areas along the Virgin River.

In the drier areas of Zion, you can find Indian paintbrush, cactus, and the sacred datura. Some people call the sacred datura the moon lily because it is white and blooms only at night. The flowers look like trumpets. Native Americans once used this plant to make medicine.

Utah's state flower, the sego lily, is also found within the park's boundaries.

Columbine flower

Cholla cactus

Three Patriarchs

Today we took a horseback trip along the Virgin River to the Court of the Patriarchs. It was named by Frederick Vining Fisher, a Methodist minister. In 1916, Rev. Fisher rode on horseback through the park for a photography trip. He spotted 3 rugged peaks lined up in a row. He called them Abraham, Isaac, and Jacob—after the Patriarchs from the Old Testament.

Three Patriarchs

Three Patriarchs

Court of the Patriarchs

Abraham is the highest tower at 6,890 feet. Rev. Fisher also gave Angels Landing and the Great White Throne their names.

A major rockslide occurred thousands of years ago near the Court of the Patriarchs. The slide was so large, it blocked off Virgin River and formed a lake 50 feet deep and 3 miles long! Later the water dried up and left a flat valley.

Mount Moroni

On our horseback ride, the guide also pointed out Mount Moroni. It stands 5,690 feet high. The Mormons named it after the angel Moroni who, it is believed, showed Joseph Smith the Book of Mormon. Smith spent many years translating the Book of Mormon and founded the Mormon religion. In 1846, Brigham Young led the Mormons west. They settled in what is now Salt Lake City, Utah.

Mount Moroni

Lady Mountain

Refrigerator Canyon

From the trail we had a good view of Lady Mountain. It is 6,540 feet high. The trail to the summit is one of the most difficult of the more than 100 miles of trails in the park. In the early 1920s, Chief Ranger Walter Ruesch developed the trail that leads from Refrigerator Canyon to Angels Landing. He put in a series of 21 switchbacks, called Walter's Wiggles. From a distance, these sharp turns look like a giant rope ladder.

From here we could also see Angels Landing—a dizzying 1,500 feet above the canyon floor! It provides some of the best views of the canyon and the river that cuts through it.

Emerald Pools Canyon

Of all the walks we have taken, I liked the walk to Emerald Pools Canyon the best. No one is allowed to wade or swim in these natural rock basins. That's so the fragile plant and aquatic life stays protected. But we still managed to get really wet! We had to walk under an alcove behind the Lower Pool to get to the Middle Pool. We got drenched walking under the waterfalls!

Emerald Pools Canyon

Emerald Pools Canyon

It was fun to try to trace the path of the water as it flows down from the top of the canyon. Sometimes it flows through large, natural funnels carved into the rock. Other times, large sheets of water spill over the edge.

The narrow trail to the last pool was steep in places, but it was worth the climb! The Upper Pool is surrounded by hanging gardens of maidenhair ferns, mosses, and wildflowers. When it rains a lot, a 300-foot-high waterfall magically appears. I got a stiff neck from bending backwards to try to see the top of the canyon—it's 1,000 feet straight up.

Great White Throne

Our next stop was the Great White Throne. Like many of the giant sandstone formations in Zion, it is red on the bottom, a chalky color in the middle, and white near the top. It rises 6,744 feet above sea level.

The ranger told us that it was once called El Gobernador, which is Spanish for "the governor." That's because it was named for a former Utah governor.

On June 24, 1927, William Evans became the first person to climb the Great White Throne. Once there, he lit several signal fires to let his friends below know that he made it. Coming down, Evans fell and was found several days later. His rescuers carried him out on horseback.

Great White Throne

Weeping Rock

Today we followed the self-guided nature trail to a place called Weeping Rock. We knew we were getting close when we heard the croaking of dozens of canyon tree frogs.

The rocks don't really cry, of course. Water travels through the soft sandstone rock until it hits a layer of shale. Since the water can't go through the shale, it seeps through to the surface, making the rock look like it is shedding big tears. The water is actually rainwater that fell on the plateau two years ago!

Weeping Rock

Weeping Rock

Wildlife

After our walk to Weeping Rock, we went to a talk by the park naturalist on the park's wildlife. The naturalist said that cougars are common here. Although they live in the canyons, they are rarely seen. The ranger said we are more likely to spot rock squirrels, mule deer, cottontail rabbits, gray foxes, elk, and lots of lizards. He said we might even see a black bear!

At the talk I learned that there are 75 species of mammals living here. There are also 32 species of amphibians and reptiles, and 8 species of fish.

Fox den

Lizard

Elk

Peregrine falcon

Of the 270 species of birds found here, some, like the canyon wren and black-headed grosbeak, are quite common. Others, like the Mexican spotted owl, are rare and endangered. The peregrine falcon was recently taken off the endangered species list. To protect its nesting sites, the National Park Service closes up to 80% of the climbing areas in the park between January and August.

The ranger told us that 70 million years ago, during the Jurassic period, giant amphibians and large, 3-toed dinosaurs roamed the park. Tracks have been found in the sandstone rock layers. The Paleo Indians, who lived in this region 11,000 years ago, hunted woolly mammoths, which also are now extinct.

25

The Pulpit and Sinawava Temple

From Weeping Rock, the road winds in a horseshoe curve around a 5,100-foot-high peak called the Organ. Trees and plants grow out of the red rock high above the ground. We also saw a pair of golden eagles swooping down to catch small rodents.

At 6,015 feet the Pulpit is even higher than the Organ. At its base are cottonwood trees. In late spring, the trees release their seeds inside a cottonlike mass. When the "cotton" covers the ground, it looks like snow!

The Pulpit

Pulpit with cottonwoods

Temple of
Sinawava

The Pulpit and
Sinawava Temple

The Pulpit is an enormous natural amphitheater and one of the best-known landmarks in the park. The prominent rock on the west side of the temple is called the Moonlight Buttress. Rock climbers consider it to be one of the best free climbs in the world!

The nearby Temple of Sinawava stands guard at the end of the scenic drive. Sinawava is the name of a powerful coyote-god of the Paiute people. From the temple we walked to the Narrows at the head of the canyon. The views of the canyon on the mile-long trail were breathtaking!

The Narrows

We talked to some hikers who had just finished walking the 16 miles through the Narrows. They looked wet and exhausted! This long canyon is 2,000 feet deep and less than 30 feet wide in most sections. The hikers told us that they had to wade through water up to their waists in some places. When it rains, there is also the danger of flash floods. That's why you need a permit to hike there.

At the end of the Narrows is the Mountain of Mystery. No one knows how the mountain got its name. I think it's because it looks so mysterious.

The Narrows

Kolob Arch

In the northwestern part of the park is Kolob Arch. It is the largest, freestanding, natural arch in the world. It is in Kolob Canyons, and it spans 310 feet. To see it, you have to hike for 7 miles from Lee Pass along the La Verkin Creek Trail. The 14-mile round trip hike can be very tiring. Because it is so far, most people camp overnight along the trail.

Kolob Terrace Road

Wildflowers

Kolob Finger Canyons

On our last day at Zion we visited the Kolob Finger Canyons. Our guidebook said this section was added to the park in 1956. We drove up the twisting Kolob Canyon Road to a picnic area. From there we had a great view of the red-rock finger canyons.

The "fingers" are actually narrow strips of land that are separated by deep canyons with walls that stretch 2,000 feet up from the canyon floor. They were carved out of the soft Navajo sandstone by moving water from 3 branches of Taylor Creek. Kolob is a Mormon word meaning "next to the throne of God."

Kolob Finger Canyons

Kolob Canyons

Horse Ranch Mountain

Just north of the finger canyons is Horse Ranch Mountain. This is the tallest peak in the entire park. It is 8,726 feet high.

I read that the mountain is capped with a basalt lava flow from the Cenozoic era. Another flow 500,000 years ago flooded and dammed the Coalpits Wash in the park's southwest corner. When the lava cooled, a large lake formed. It eventually filled with sediment and dried up. Crater Hill, a cinder cone near Coalpits Wash, is a reminder of the last volcanic activity in the park.

I really hate to see this trip end. It's been so much fun! But I can't wait to get home to show everyone my photos of the colored canyons, the river, and all the strange rock formations.

Horse Ranch Mountain

Glossary

Alcove a place that is set back from the main area.

Amphitheater a bowl-shaped land form with steep slopes rising from a flat or gently sloping area.

Buttress a part of a mountain or hill that juts out.

Endangered species a plant or animal that is in danger of becoming extinct.

Erosion the process of gradual wearing away.

Geologist someone who studies earth's layers of soil and rock.

Seep to flow slowly.

Shale a rock that is made from hardened layers of clay or mud.

Summit the highest point.

Switchback a road or trail that follows a zigzag course up a steep slope.

For More Information

Books

Fradin, Dennis Brindell. *Utah* (From Sea to Shining Sea). Danbury, CT: Children's Press, 1993.

Geist, Valerius. Michael Francis. *Mule Deer Country.* Minocqua, WI: NorthWord Press, 1999.

Silverstein, Alvin, Virginia, and Robert. *The Peregrine Falcon.* Brookfield, CT: Millbrook Press, 1995.

Web Sites

Geology Field Notes: Zion National Park

This National Park Service web site features information on and photos of the park's geology— www.aqd.nps.gov/grd/parks/zion/#relsites

Zion National Park

This DesertUSA web site provides information on the park's geography and climate— www.desertusa.com/zion/du-znpmap.html

Index